Valentine Fun

Messner Holiday Library
Valentine Fun
by Judith Hoffman Corwin

Julian Messner   New York

Design by Judith Hoffman Corwin

Library of Congress Cataloging in Publication Data

(The Messner holiday library)
Summary: Instructions for making greeting cards,
decorations, gift wrappings, presents, and things to
eat for Valentine's Day with easily available materials.
Also gives a brief history of the holiday and some of
the customs connected with it.
1. Valentine decorations—Juvenile literature.
2. Valentines—Juvenile literature. 3. Cookery—
Juvenile literature. [1. Valentine decorations.
2. Valentines. 3. Cookery. 4. Handicraft.
5. Holidays] I. Title. II. Series.

TT900.V34C67 1982   745.594'1   82-60647
ISBN 0-671-45945-7

For Jules Arthur and Oliver Jamie, my Valentines

MESSNER BOOKS BY JUDITH HOFFMAN CORWIN

The Messner Holiday Library: Valentine Fun

The Messner Holiday Library: Christmas Fun

Contents

FOR YOU!

Valentine's Day, February 14, is a very special holiday because it is for people to tell people that they care for them. Rosy-cheeked winged cherubs, plump hearts, delicate lace, and beautiful birds and flowers warm the heart as well as the cold winter's day.

Valentine Fun will help you to enjoy Valentine's Day in many ways. It is full of ideas for making greeting cards, decorations, gift wrappings, presents, and good things to eat. Best of all, you will be able to make everything yourself, using mostly things that you can find around the house. You will also learn why we do some of the things we do on Valentine's Day.

When you are making the projects remember to follow the directions carefully, be patient, and most of all enjoy yourself!

Valentine's Day

Nobody knows exactly why we celebrate Valentine's Day or when it all started. Some scholars think that Valentine's Day was originally the *Lupercalia*, a joyous Roman feast for lovers celebrated around what is now February 14 on our calendar. When the Romans became Christians, the *Lupercalia* was replaced by a holiday in honor of St. Valentine, a Christian martyr. St. Valentine, who died more than 1700 years ago, is now popularly considered to be the patron saint of lovers. And St. Valentine's Day has become the time to tell people you like them by sending greetings—called, of course, "valentines."

People have always made their own valentines even though the first commercial greeting cards in the United States were manufactured in the 1840s. Examples of early handmade valentines—some more than 100 years old—still exist. Some are quite fancy and have fold-outs, satin ribbons, and lace. They are decorated with hearts, flowers, and birds. You will have your chance to equal the best of these antiques when you make some of the projects in this book.

Before You Begin

Make your own pattern

Directions for most of the projects in this book include patterns for you to make an exact copy of what is shown. You don't want to cut up the book, so make your own patterns with tracing paper. Begin by placing a piece of tracing paper over the pattern to be transferred from the book. Using a pencil with soft lead, trace over the outline of what is in the book. When you have finished, cut out what you have drawn on the tracing paper. Now you have your own pattern.

Using your pattern

Pin your pattern or hold it down carefully on the paper or fabric you have chosen to work with. Draw around the edges of the pattern. Then lift up the tracing paper pattern and go on with the other instructions for your project.

Materials you will need

The basic materials you need are readily available from stationery stores and art supply shops: cardboard, oaktag, heavy white paper, and colored paper. Extras like cloth and bits of lace may be found at home or at fabric departments in stores. For details or accents you'll need colored markers (waterproof), pencils, or watercolors. You will also need a sharp pair of scissors and a good brand of white glue.

Preparing a work area

Before starting to work, make sure that all your supplies are at hand and that everything is neat and clean. Cover your work surface with newspaper to protect it from glue. By the way, when you work with glue always spread a thin, even coat. A thin coat sticks better and is less likely to cause the paper to buckle.

For the cooking projects you will need an adult to help you with the stove.

Most projects in *Valentine Fun* can be made quite easily. Some may prove more of a challenge—but you can do them all. Have fun!

10

Teddy Bear Party Invitation

Valentine's Day is such a special time of year, there are bound to be lots of parties. You'll probably want to have one yourself. Here's a fun invitation to make—one that can be hung up as well.

MATERIALS:

white oaktag
square of red felt
black felt tip marker
string, hole punch
scissors, pencil
business-size envelopes

METHOD:

1. Trace the patterns, then place the boy and girl teddy bears on oaktag, and the heart on felt.

2. Cut out the oaktag and the red felt along the pattern lines.

3. Checking the illustrations, paint on the teddy bears' clothes and features with the felt tip marker. Glue the heart in place.

4. On the reverse side write out your invitation. Be sure to include the time, place, and request to reply (r.s.v.p.) so you will know how many guests you will have.

5. Make a hole with the hole punch in the top of the head, as shown, and pull a 6″ length of string through it. Knot the string.

6. These teddy bear invitations will fit into a plain business-size envelope. Decorate your envelopes by drawing on hearts.

12

Quick Chocolate Fudge Sweet

This delicious fudge is easy to make and great to eat yourself or to give to someone who has a "sweet tooth" on Valentine's Day.

INGREDIENTS YOU WILL NEED:

1 lb. box confectioner's 10–X powdered sugar
½ cup cocoa
¼ teaspoon salt
6 tablespoons butter
4 tablespoons milk
1 tablespoon vanilla extract
1 six oz. package semisweet chocolate pieces
1 cup chopped walnuts
1 tablespoon butter for greasing loaf pan

UTENSILS YOU WILL NEED:

9" × 5" loaf pan
measuring spoons and cup
spatula
knife
medium-size saucepan ⎫
large-size saucepan ⎭ or a double boiler

DIRECTIONS:

1. You will need to use a double boiler for this recipe. If you do not have one, fill a small saucepan ¼ full with cold water and put a larger saucepan on top. (The saucepan must be just big enough to fit halfway down the bottom pot so that it rests on water.) A double boiler is necessary so that the chocolate cooks over water instead of a flame. Otherwise your chocolate will burn.

2. Combine all the ingredients, except the chocolate pieces and nuts, in the top container of the double boiler.

3. Allow the water in the bottom of the double boiler to simmer while you stir the mixture until it is completely smooth.

4. Add the chocolate pieces and nuts.

5. Spread candy quickly in the buttered 9" × 5" loaf pan.

6. Put into refrigerator for several hours and then cut into squares.

13

Cheery Cherry Lemonade

Lemons and cherries and ginger ale combine to make a bubbly fun drink.

INGREDIENTS YOU WILL NEED:

6 lemons
1 large bottle of ginger ale
1 quart of ice water
2 cups sugar
1 small bottle of red cherries

UTENSILS YOU WILL NEED:

large bowl
ladle
squeezer

DIRECTIONS:

1. Cut lemons in half and squeeze. Pour juice and lemon rinds into bowl.

2. Add sugar, water, ginger ale, and cherries.

3. Stir well and serve with ladle.

Hot Chocolate To Warm Your Heart

A marshmallow with a cherry on top makes this a festive drink.

INGREDIENTS YOU WILL NEED:

2 cups chocolate syrup
2 quarts of milk
marshmallows
cherries

UTENSILS YOU WILL NEED:

large saucepan
stirring spoon
toothpicks

DIRECTIONS:

1. For each cup you will be serving, spear a marshmallow with a cherry on a toothpick.

2. Put milk in saucepan with chocolate syrup and stir to blend.

3. Continue stirring until mixture comes to a boil. Remove from heat immediately or it will boil over and mess up the stove!

4. Pour chocolate into cups and then add marshmallows.

Heart-Shaped Sugar Cookies

A crispy vanilla heart-shaped cookie, topped with sugar.

INGREDIENTS:

2½ cups pre-sifted all-purpose flour
¾ cup (1½ sticks) butter, softened
½ teaspoon salt
1¼ cups sugar
1 egg
2 teaspoons vanilla extract
4 tablespoons flour (to prepare working surface)
extra butter to grease cookie sheets
½ cup sugar to sprinkle on cookies

UTENSILS:

small mixing bowl
large mixing bowl
measuring spoons and cups
spatula
cookie sheets
waxed paper

DIRECTIONS:

1. Combine the flour and salt in the small mixing bowl.

2. Beat the butter, sugar, and egg in the large mixing bowl until light and fluffy. Add vanilla.

3. Stir in the flour mixture. You will now have a stiff dough. Wrap this dough in wax paper and chill for several hours. If you do not want to use all the dough at once, you can leave some of the dough in the refrigerator for another day.

4. Make your cookies in a heart shape. Use a cookie cutter, or if you do not have one, you can make a heart-shaped cardboard pattern. Roll the dough to a ¼" thickness on a lightly floured surface, and stamp the hearts with the cookie cutter or cut them out with a knife around the cardboard.

5. Place the cookies 1" apart on a lightly greased cookie sheet and sprinkle them with sugar.

6. Bake in the oven at 350° for 8 minutes or until the cookies are lightly browned at the edges. Remove with a spatula and let cool.

16

Fortune Cookies

These small cookies with your fortune tucked inside will entertain your friends at a Valentine party or just about any time. They are easy to make because you use store-bought refrigerator cookies that just need slicing and baking. Here goes!

MATERIALS:

1 roll of refrigerator cookies
red sugar (for decorating the cookies)
knife
cookie sheets
8½" × 11" white paper
felt tip marker, scissors

METHOD:

1. Cut the piece of paper into ½" by 2" rectangles. Write a silly valentine message or fortune on each piece of paper. Here are some examples: "Beware of Cupid"; "Avoid heartburn"; "You will love . . . cookies!" Fold the message in half after you have finished writing it.

2. Make the refrigerator cookies by following the directions given on the package—but slice them a little thinner than is suggested. You may need help from an adult with this.

3. After you have sliced the cookies, but before you bake them, fold the dough in half and slip the fortune inside. Seal the dough by pressing the edges together.

4. As the package directs, put the cookies onto the cookie sheet, sprinkle them with the red sugar, and bake for the suggested time.

17

Fresh-From-The-Oven Homemade Cinnamon Bread

This bread has a wonderful smell and will be a welcome Valentine's gift. Wrap it as suggested and include the recipe so the person to whom you give the bread can make it later on.

INGREDIENTS YOU WILL NEED:

½ cup butter, softened (1 stick)
1 cup granulated white sugar
½ cup brown sugar
2 eggs
1 cup sour cream
2 cups flour
¼ cup milk
1 teaspoon vanilla extract
1½ teaspoons baking powder
1 teaspoon baking soda
½ teaspoon salt
1 tablespoon ground cinnamon
extra butter for greasing the pan

UTENSILS YOU WILL NEED:

9″ × 5″ × 3″ loaf pan
large mixing bowl
rubber spatula
measuring cups and spoons
2 small mixing bowls
knife
spoon
toothpick
potholders
wire rack

DIRECTIONS:

1. Set oven temperature to 350°. Grease the loaf pan with a little shortening.

2. Place the butter and white sugar in the large mixing bowl and beat until fluffy.

3. Add the eggs and vanilla and beat until completely combined.

4. Mixing well, add the sour cream and the milk.

5. In one of the small bowls mix the flour, baking powder, baking soda, and salt.

6. Now make a batter by combining the flour mixture with the butter mixture in the large bowl.

7. In the second small bowl mix together the brown sugar and the cinnamon.

8. Pour half of the batter into the loaf pan, then sprinkle the cinnamon mixture on top of the batter. Make swirls in the batter with the spatula to combine both mixtures. Pour the remaining batter into the loaf pan.

9. Put the loaf pan into the oven and bake for one hour or until the cake tests "done" when you insert a toothpick into the center.

10. Using potholders, remove the loaf pan from the oven. Let cool for 10 minutes on a wire rack.

11. Run a knife along all four sides of the bread to loosen it from the pan. Turn the pan upside down and gently tap to remove the bread. Let bread completely cool on the wire rack before slicing. To keep the bread fresh put it into a plastic bag and tie the end securely with a plastic twist.

Apple-Of-My-Eye Applesauce Cake

This yummy cake will quickly disappear from the serving plate.

INGREDIENTS YOU WILL NEED:

1¾ cups white flour, sifted
½ teaspoon salt
1 teaspoon baking soda
1 teaspoon cinnamon
½ cup butter, softened
1 cup brown sugar (pack the sugar down into the cup)
1 egg
1 cup applesauce
4 medium-size apples, peeled
4 tablespoons confectioner's sugar
2 tablespoons butter to grease the tube pan

UTENSILS YOU WILL NEED:

9″ tube pan
large mixing bowl
medium-size bowl
spatula, sifter
measuring cups and spoons

DIRECTIONS:

1. Combine the flour, salt, baking soda, and cinnamon in the medium-size bowl. Put aside.

2. Using the large bowl, beat the butter until it is soft and fluffy, gradually adding the brown sugar.

3. Beat the egg into the butter mixture.

4. Now combine the flour mixture (medium bowl) with the butter mixture and stir.

5. Peel the apples and cut them into small chunks about ½″ in size. Add them and the applesauce to the batter.

6. Grease the tube pan and pour the batter into the pan. Bake at 350° for 50–60 minutes. After the cake has cooled, transfer it to a plate and sift confectioner's sugar on top.

Woven Paper Heart

Red and white woven paper basket holds a secret valentine message for someone special.

MATERIALS:

1 sheet red and 2 sheets white construction paper
ruler, pencil, glue

METHOD:

1. Cut a 10¼" square of white paper. Fold it in half, then fold in half again.

2. Mark the top of the heart on the edges of the square away from the folds.

3. On the first heart, measure four lines, ¾" apart, from the folded edge toward the top of the heart (see diagram). Cut on these lines, leaving the curved part of the heart solid, as shown.

4. Now cut a piece of red paper 3 ¾" × 6 ½". Using the full-size heart as a pattern, cut one end of the red paper in the shape of a half-heart. Mark three lines ¾" apart and cut from the bottom up, leaving the top solid and uncut.

5. Now weave the red half-heart into the white heart, over and under. Cut two slits at the bottom of the white heart from the red ends and fold all the extra length of red inside the heart. Glue curve of red heart to white.

6. Glue the open sides of the heart together, as shown, to form a basket.

7. To make a handle for the basket, fold a 6"

× 1" strip of white paper lengthwise and glue together. Attach this to the center of the basket.

8. On a 2" square of white paper write your valentine message and put it into the heart basket.

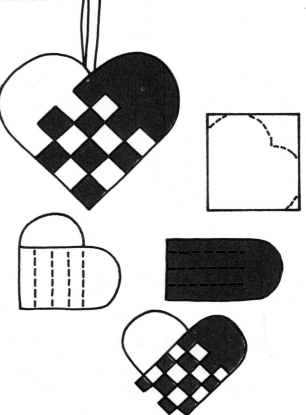

22

She Loves Me, She Loves Me Not Doll

This doll is made from a wooden spoon and has two faces. One side has a happy face and the other a sad one.

MATERIALS:

wooden spoon
acrylic paints
brushes
pencil
tracing paper
¼ yard unbleached muslin
red felt tip marker
6 cotton balls
thread, needle, straight pins
½ yard lace
¼ yard ribbon

METHOD:

1. Checking the illustration, with the pencil draw the face and hair on each side of the wooden spoon. Now go over the pencil lines with acrylic paints.

2. Follow the diagram to make a pattern for the dress. Use this pattern to cut two pieces from the unbleached muslin. Draw hearts all over the muslin with the red felt tip marker.

3. Stitch the shoulders with the patterned sides of the fabric facing each other, leaving a 3" neck opening.

4. Pin the sides together, leaving a ¼" seam allowance. Now sew along the sides, turning stitching at underarms to sew sleeves.

5. To make arms for the doll, draw the pattern onto tracing paper, cut out, and then pin to muslin. Add ¼" seam allowance around all edges. Sew together and then turn everything right side out. Stuff the arms firmly with cotton balls—3 in each arm. Sew open end closed.

6. Cut lace to fit the sleeve and neck edges. Glue the lace to the muslin.

7. Sew each arm into sleeve of dress, so the hands extend beyond the lace edges.

8. Slip the dress onto the spoon, tie in place at waist and neck with ribbon. Glue lace along bottom edge of dress.

23

Hoot, Hoot Oliver Owl

Oliver Owl gives a hoot for his special valentine. This stuffed friend carries a nice message: "I really give a hoot for you!"

MATERIALS:

½ yard unbleached muslin (this should make at least 4 owls)
polyester batting
white sewing thread
straight pins
needle, thread, scissors
pencil, felt tip marker, wax crayons
waxed paper, white paper, iron

METHOD:

1. Make a pattern for the owl by tracing the design given.

2. Fold the muslin in half. Place the pattern on top of the muslin and trace around the outline with a pencil. Remove the pattern, and pin the folded piece of cloth together so that it holds steady. About ¼" out from the pattern line, cut the pattern, leaving the pins in.

3. Checking the illustration, draw the details of the owl with a pencil. When you are satisfied with what you have drawn, draw over the pencil line with a felt tip marker.

4. Color the owl with crayons. The back of the owl can be one solid color, or you can repeat the feather design from the front.

5. Unfold the owl and place it crayoned side up on an ironing board. Place a piece of wax paper on top and gently iron. Ironing sets the color and makes it shiny. You may need an adult to help you with this.

6. With the sides that have been colored facing each other, pin the owl together.

7. Sew the two sides together with a ½" seam all around, leaving a 2" opening for the stuffing to go through.

8. Clip the curves with your scissors. This keeps the curves from puckering after the owl has been stuffed.

9. Turn the owl right side out and stuff. Stitch up the opening.

10. Fold a 2" square of paper in half, write "I give a hoot for you" and attach it to the owl with a string as shown.

It might be fun to make several different-colored owls. This project could also be a popular one to make and sell at school to raise money for a party.

26

Lovebirds and Hearts Mobile

The slightest breeze will move these Valentine lovebirds surrounded by hearts. The mobile is easily made from white oaktag and, hung up in your room or classroom, it will delight all who see it.

MATERIALS:

tracing paper
pencil
white oaktag
red felt
colored felt tip markers

wire hanger
white thread, needle
glue
scissors
12 small white buttons

METHOD:

1. Trace the patterns for the bird and the heart. Transfer the bird pattern onto the oaktag and the heart pattern onto the felt. You will have to make two birds and three hearts.

2. Cut the oaktag along the pattern lines to make the birds. Cut the hearts out of the felt.

3. Draw the designs on the birds first in pencil and then with the felt tip markers. Both sides of the birds must be decorated so that whichever way they move they look beautiful.

4. Checking the illustration, glue the buttons onto the birds on both sides.

5. Using a needle, make a hole in the birds and hearts, as shown in the illustration.

6. Run a piece of thread through the holes and knot to secure the thread. Attach each bird—they should be facing each other— and heart to the hanger as shown in the il-

lustration. Secure with a knot. Now your lovebird mobile is ready to hang up in your room.

Come Alive Valentine

Here's a super valentine for a special friend—a real live self-portrait! You will need a friend's help for this project and then you can help him or her do a self-portrait in turn.

MATERIALS:

needle
thread
scissors
cotton batting
belt snaps
fabric—for small size, 13″ × 4″. For large size, 1 yard—*36″* wide.

METHOD:

1. Cut a large enough piece of sheet so that you can lie down on it. If you are using newspaper, tape pages together until you get the proper size. Now tape the sheet or newspaper to the floor at all corners.

2. Lie down on the sheet or newspaper and have your friend draw around the outline of your whole body with a pencil.

3. Now you can add the details of your clothes, hair, and other features with the felt tip pens—and don't forget the heart!

4. You can either cut out your shape along the pencil line or leave it on the sheet, going over the pencil line with a black felt tip pen.

5. Sign your masterpiece and give it to a friend!

Sidney, The Garden Of Eden Snake

Sidney the Snake comes in two sizes—a large, six-foot one, and a small one, 13" long. Sidney can hang around your neck while you do your homework, or you can "coil up" with him as a comfortable pillow!

MATERIALS YOU WILL NEED:

thread, needle, scissors
cotton batting
belt snaps
fabric—for small size, 13" × 4". For large size, 1 yard—36" wide.

METHOD (To make either the small or large Sidney):

1. To start, cut a length of fabric, preferably green, 13" long by 4" wide for the small Sidney, 12" wide and six feet long for the large one. You will have to piece the fabric together to get a length of six feet, so first cut 12"-wide strips and then sew six together to make a total of six feet.

2. With right sides together, fold the snake in half along the length.

3. One end will be the head, the other the tail. Both ends should be curved, as shown in the illustration. The tail should be slightly thinner than the rest of the body.

4. Sew the seam ½ inch (¼ inch for the small version) from the rough edge all the way down to the tail section. Leave the tail end open so you can stuff the snake, about 4 inches for the large snake, or one inch for the small snake.

5. Turn the snake right side out and stuff. When finished, sew the opening closed.

6. Using red felt, make the snake's features. Cut a forked tongue and two eyes and glue them in place.

7. Use the red felt to make a heart for the final touch—Sidney has feelings you know!

I Love You

Cuddly Cupid

This small winged friend will delight everyone who sees him. You can scent him with perfume and give him as a gift or hang him so he can fly freely.

MATERIALS:

2 squares pink felt for cupid's body
1 square white felt for wings
scraps of felt for hair (yellow), eyes (black), mouth (red)
scrap of calico for shorts
polyester batting
pink and white sewing thread
needle, straight pins
pencil, paper
glue, scissors

METHOD:

1. Make a pattern for the cupid, his wings, and his shorts by tracing the designs given.

2. Place the two squares of pink felt on top of each other. Place the pattern for the cupid on top of them and trace around the outline with a pencil. Remove the pattern and pin the two pieces of felt together so they hold steady. Cut the pattern on the line that you have just drawn, leaving the pins in.

3. Repeat this with the patterns for the wings and the shorts by folding the white felt and the calico in half. In this way you will make two wings and the two halves of cupid's shorts.

4. Cut out the patterns for the hair, eyes, and mouth, and glue in place.

5. Sew around the outside edge of the cupid with the pink thread, leaving the pins in.

Leave a 1½" opening for the stuffing to go through.

6. Now stuff the cupid. If he is to be scented, insert a perfume-soaked ball of cotton as you begin to stuff. Stitch up the opening.

7. Sew around the outside of the wings with the white thread, leaving the pins in. Leave a small opening for the stuffing to go through. Put a small amount of stuffing in each *side* of the wings—don't put any stuffing in the centers of the wings. Sew the wings in place.

8. Glue the shorts to the front and back of cupid.

9. Cut out a small heart from a piece of white paper. Write "I love you" on it, and glue onto cupid.

10. If you want to hang your cupid up, sew a bright thread through the center of his wings where they are attached to his body.

Parachute Jumper Valentine

With this parachute jumper you can have a contest with your friends to see whose jumper takes the longest trip to earth in search of his or her valentine.

MATERIALS:

wooden clothes pin
cotton handkerchief
poster paints
paintbrush
container of water to wash the brushes
clear nail polish
string—4 feet
fabric
pencil, ruler

METHOD:

1. To make the parachute jumper, follow the illustration to paint the face, hair, tee shirt, jeans and shoes. You can make a boy or a girl parachute jumper.

2. After the paint has dried, seal it with clear nail polish and let dry thoroughly.

3. To make the parachute, first cut four lengths of string 12″ long each. Then paint a red heart on each corner of the handkerchief and one in the center. Tie one piece of string to each corner of the handkerchief.

4. Now tie the four loose ends to the neck of the parachute jumper. Roll up your parachute, then toss it as high in the air as you can. It will come down just like a real parachute.

34

Lacy Fashion Plate Valentine

Lace and ribbon are an important part of Valentine's Day. Here's a chance to dress this lovely old-fashioned lady and put ribbons and lace all around her. Fancy wrapping paper or interesting fabric are used for the background and it's finished off with a lace border and flowers.

MATERIALS:

cardboard or oaktag, about 8½" × 11"
colored wrapping paper
tracing paper
carbon paper
white paper
bits of fabric, lace, and ribbon
small buttons
glue, scissors
felt tip markers, pink colored pencil
pencil

METHOD:

1. First, trace the lady's body and the flowers onto tracing paper.

2. Now put this tracing on a sheet of carbon paper placed over the white paper you will be using to make your valentine.

3. Gently tape the three sheets down onto your working surface at the top and bottom. This will prevent the papers from sliding around as you draw over the design again with a pencil. Make sure your pencil is not too sharp or the paper will tear. Press firmly and evenly. When you lift off the tracing and carbon papers you should have a copy of the lady and flowers on the white paper. Re-trace the carbon lines with a black felt tip marker.

4. Now prepare the background by covering the cardboard with wrapping paper or fabric. Use two different patterns, as shown.

5. Checking the illustration for placement, glue the lady's body onto the background.

6. Make patterns for the blouse and the skirt with tracing paper.

7. Cut the blouse out of some interesting fabric. The sleeves should be cut separately so you can see that they are properly attached. Glue the blouse in place. Some lace should be added around the neckline, and a small bead should be glued to the center of the lace.

8. The skirt can be made from a fabric that goes with the blouse, or you can use solid color material and draw designs, as shown, with a felt tip marker. Pucker the skirt at the waist, as shown, by folding. Now glue it in place along the waistline, along the sides, and along the hem.

9. Cut a piece of narrow ribbon the width of the waist and glue it in place. You can also make a small bow of ribbon and glue it to the center of the waist. Glue lace, paper doily material, or lengths of yarn to the hem.

10. Take a pink colored pencil or a felt tip marker and add color to the cheeks of the lady. Color in the flowers underneath her.

11. To finish, cut lace or pieces of a paper doily and glue them around the outside of your valentine.

Catherine Cat Valentine

An amusing stuffed cat valentine. Write your valentine message on Catherine's reverse side.

MATERIALS:

½ yard unbleached muslin (this should make at least 4 cats)
polyester batting
white sewing thread
straight pins
needle, thread
scissors
pencil, felt tip marker
wax crayons
waxed paper, tracing paper
iron

METHOD:

1. Make a pattern for the cat by tracing the design given.

2. Fold the muslin in half. Place the pattern on top of the muslin and trace around the outline of it with a pencil. Remove the pattern and pin the folded piece of cloth together so it holds steady. About ¼" away from the pattern line, cut out the pattern, leaving the pins in.

3. Checking the illustration, draw the details of the cat on the muslin with a pencil. When you are satisfied with what you have drawn, draw over the pencil line with a felt tip marker.

4. Color the cat with crayons. Check the illustration for an idea of where to write your message on the back of the cat.

5. Unfold the cat and place, crayoned side up, on an ironing board. Put a piece of waxed paper on top and gently iron to set the color and make it shiny. You may need an adult to help you with this.

6. With the sides that have been colored facing each other, pin the cat together.

7. Sew the two sides together on the pattern line, leaving the pins in. Leave a 1½" opening for the stuffing to go through.

8. Clip the curves with your scissors. This keeps the curves from puckering after the cat has been stuffed.

9. Turn the cat inside out and stuff. If you would like your cat to be scented, insert a cotton ball that has been soaked in perfume into the center. Stitch up the opening.

10. It would be fun to make several of the cats in different colors. This project could also be a popular one to make and sell at school to raise money for a valentine party. You could leave the message side blank and whoever buys the cat could write in his or her own special message.

Secret Admirer Codes

Here are two codes for you to use to send valentine messages to a friend. Be sure to give your friend a copy of the code. He or she will then be able to decode what you have sent and will also be able to send messages in code to you.

MATERIALS:

paper
pencil or felt tip marker

METHOD:

1. Write out each of the codes so you have a copy that you can carry with you easily.

2. When you write a message in code, make sure that you leave a little extra space between each word so that it's easier to decode the messages. Later on when you and your friends have become experts you can try running the words together so that they become harder to decode.

3. The first code is made up of symbols—see the illustration. The second code is made by substituting odd numbers for each letter of the alphabet—for instance, 1 stands for A, 3 stands for B, 5 stands for C, and so on through the alphabet.

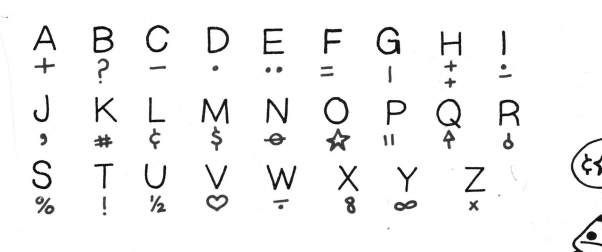

Hearts and Sweethearts Jewelry

You can make great jewelry to wear or give as Valentine's Day presents. The jewelry is made from flour clay, and patterns are given for a heart, cupid, flower, parrot, teddy bear, pencil, mouse, turtle, frog, pig, and kangaroo—all of which can be made out of one recipe.

INGREDIENTS:

2 cups flour
1 cup salt
1 cup water

UTENSILS YOU WILL NEED:

measuring cup
large bowl
cookie sheet

MATERIALS:

tracing paper
cardboard
pencil, scissors
acrylic paints
shellac, brushes
toothpick
colored thread or ribbon
knife, glue

METHOD:

1. Mix the flour and salt together in a large bowl. Then add the water a little at a time, mixing it in. When all the water is used up, mix the dough well with your hands. This is called "kneading."

2. Continue kneading the dough until it is smooth.

3. Put some flour on a clean working surface and then roll the dough to about ¼" thick. (The dough will expand slightly when it is baked.)

4. Trace the pattern of the ornament you want from the book, and transfer it to the cardboard. Cut out the cardboard pattern.

5. Place the cardboard cutout on the dough. Hold the cardboard down with one hand and then use your knife carefully to cut the dough around the pattern.

6. Roll small pieces of dough for eyes, cheeks, and other features. Put some dough through a sieve (strainer) to make hair. Moisten the ornament with a drop of water, then put on the dough decorations. Moistening makes them stick better.

7. The heart, cupid, and flower can be made into necklaces by making a hole at the top with a toothpick so that they can be strung on colored thread or ribbon. The parrot, teddy bear, pencil, mouse, and kangaroo can be made into pins by glueing a safety pin to the unpainted side.

8. Set the oven at 325°. Place the ornaments on a cookie sheet at least 1" apart and bake until lightly browned. It takes about 30–40

minutes, but keep checking the oven to make sure that the ornaments aren't burning along the edges.

9. Using a potholder to protect your hand, remove the cookie sheet from the oven. When the ornaments are cool, take them off the cookie sheet.

10. Decorate your ornaments with acrylic paints (see patterns).

11. When the ornaments are dry, cover them completely with shellac to keep out any moisture and to preserve them.

Valentine Tee Shirts

This charming butterfly decorates a plain white tee shirt and is a perfect thing to wear on Valentine's Day. There are two other designs for you to try, also.

MATERIALS:

white cotton tee shirt
waterproof felt tip markers (in bright colors and black)
cardboard
tracing paper
carbon paper
pencil
tape

METHOD:

1. First trace the butterfly design, using tracing paper.

2. Now lay the tee shirt onto your work surface so that it is perfectly flat, with the front facing you. Slip a piece of cardboard into the shirt. This will prevent the ink from the markers going onto the back of the shirt.

3. Place a piece of carbon paper on top of the tee shirt and tape it down. Now tape the traced butterfly design on top of the carbon paper. Check the illustration for placement.

4. Draw over the design firmly with a pencil. Then remove the tracing and carbon paper from the tee shirt, leaving the cardboard in place. Now draw over the outline of the design with a black felt tip marker.

5. Color in the design with the bright felt tip markers. The hearts should be red, the body of the butterfly green, eyes blue, and wings orange, yellow, and purple. Experiment with your color choices. You may wish to draw some hearts around the neckline and along the edges of the sleeves to give your shirt an extra valentine flair.

50

Window Valentine

A surprise is behind the door and each of the five windows of this little house. This makes an interesting variety of valentine.

MATERIALS:

oaktag
white paper
1 small white button
carbon paper, pencil
tracing paper
razor, scissors, ruler
felt tip markers
glue, tape

METHOD:

1. First trace the design of the house with tracing paper.

2. Place a sheet of carbon paper over a sheet of white paper. Now place the traced design over the carbon paper. Gently tape the three sheets down onto your work surface at the top and bottom. This will prevent the papers from sliding around. Draw over the design again with a pencil (not too sharp!) making sure to press firmly and evenly. When you lift off the tracing and carbon papers you should have a copy of the house design on the white paper.

3. Now cut out the house with a scissors. To make the windows and door open, use a razor blade to cut along the broken lines carefully. You may need the help of an adult for this stage of the project.

5. Now crease along the fold lines to make the windows and door open. Glue the button onto the door for the door knob.

6. Place the paper house on a sheet of oaktag and trace around the outlines, including the outlines of the door and windows (open them first). Now cut out the house (but not the door and windows) from the oaktag.

7. Now transfer the designs for the boy or girl and the lovebirds, lion, dog, cat, and sun onto the oaktag house by following steps 1-3 above—using the oaktag instead of white paper. Position the boy and girl carefully in the doors and the animals and sun in the windows before pressing down on the carbon paper.

8. After the designs have been transferred, go over the carbon lines with a felt tip marker. Now color them in as you like.

9. Glue the paper house on top of the oaktag house, making sure the windows and door of the paper house fit neatly over the designs on the oaktag house. Only small amounts of glue should be used. The glue should be placed on the oaktag house along its outline and around the outline of the windows and the door. Be careful not to spread the glue into the window or door openings since this will glue the paper door and windows shut!

10. As a finishing touch you can draw in curtains, window frames, or flowers, as shown. The window with the sun behind it also has room for a valentine message.

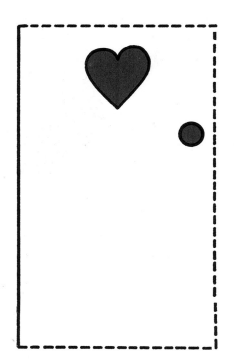

53

Good Buddy Bunny Valentine

This bunny has a real cotton tail, a satin ribbon bow, and a mirror attached to him which will reflect the person that the sender loves!

MATERIALS:

yellow oaktag
pink felt
black, fine line felt tip marker
cotton balls
small mirror
7″ length of satin ribbon
glue, scissors, pencil, tracing paper

METHOD:

1. Make a pattern for the bunny by tracing the design given. Use the pattern to cut the bunny out of the yellow oaktag.

2. Cut pink felt to fit the bunny's nose and the insides of his ears. Glue in place.

3. Draw in the bunny's eyes, whiskers, and paws with a black, fine line felt tip marker.

4. Make a bow with the ribbon and glue in place.

5. Glue a cotton ball in place for the bunny's tail.

6. Glue the mirror in place, and above it write "I love you!"

Victoria And Vincent

These paper dolls are made from oaktag, and their clothes are made from paper, scraps of fabric, and lace. You can even string a necklace of tiny beads for Victoria. They can be dressed in their costumes from the early 1900s or in a tee shirt and jeans.

MATERIALS:

oaktag (for the dolls)
heavy cardboard (for stands on which to place the dolls)
tracing paper
white paper
bits of fabric and lace
small buttons
tiny beads
glue
scissors
pencil
felt tip markers in bright colors
fine line felt tip marker (black)
tape

METHOD:

1. First place a sheet of tracing paper over Victoria, Vincent, and their clothes. Trace.

2. Now place a sheet of carbon paper over the oaktag or the white paper that you will be using to make the dolls and their clothes. On top of the carbon paper place the tracing paper with the design drawn on it.

3. Gently tape the three sheets down onto your working surface at the top and bottom. This will prevent the papers from sliding around as you draw. Draw over design.

4. Remove the tracing paper and carbon paper. With the black fine line felt tip marker, draw over the designs. Cut out. Add color with the other markers. Bits of lace and fabric and a string of beads can be added as you wish.

5. Make a pattern for the stand and cut it out of the heavy cardboard. Insert the dolls in the stands.

59

Flowers Have Special Meanings

Flowers are lovely to look at, delightful to smell, and a gift to the world as they grace our paths, meadows and gardens. Each flower also has a particular meaning. A rose means love, and is the most popular flower on Valentine's Day.

Here are some flower designs for you to have fun with. They can be used to decorate a tee shirt or stationery, repeated to make wrapping paper, made into a necklace, or pasted on a card with scraps of colored paper, fabric and lace added. Enjoy letting your imagination run free.

Rose—love
Red Tulip—declaration of love
Yellow Tulip—hopeless love
Multi-colored Tulip—beautiful eyes
Daisy—innocence
Lily—purity, sweetness
Appleblossom—preference
Scarlet Red Poppy—fantastic extravagance
White Poppy—sleep that cures a broken heart
Marigold—grief
Buttercup—ingratitude
Daffodil—regard
Honeysuckle—generous and devoted affection
Purple Lilac—first emotion of love
Blue Violet—faithfulness
Sunflower—thoughtfulness
Strawberry—esteem and love
Dahlia—instability
Forget Me Not—remembrance, true love
Iris—message
Red Carnation—alas! my poor heart
Striped Carnation—refusal
Yellow Carnation—disdain

Index